The Christmas Candle

The Christmas Candle

By Pat Ganger

GOM
PRESS
An Imprint of Gom Publishing
Columbus, Ohio

PRESS

An imprint of Gom Publishing, LLC
P.O. Box 211110, Columbus, Ohio 43221

Phone: 866.466.2608
Email: communications@gompublishing.com
Internet: **www.gompublishing.com**

ISBN 978-1-932966-62-6

First Gom Press printing: October 2008

1 3 5 7 9 10 8 6 4 2

This book is printed on acid-free paper.

Harry Long

Chapter 1

It was two years since Harry Long's wife had died, and he sorely missed her quiet companionship. They had been married forty-three years, almost half of Harry's lifetime. It was not that he was unused to being alone. Harry had been a lighthouse keeper for over thirty-five years, a job thought by many to be a lonely existence, but one Harry found suited him admirably. He found the wind and the sea powerful evidence of a powerful God, one Harry had come to know intimately during those solitary years in the lighthouse.

Sitting down to a simple lunch of canned soup and a cup of tea, Harry's mind drifted back to the day he and Martha first came to what soon became to them "their lighthouse" and the only home they had known or wanted. He missed his wife's good homemade soup, but not being much of a cook, Harry had to settle for the commercial brands. Cooking had always been Martha's gift, and she enjoyed preparing delicious meals for them to enjoy each evening when their work was done and they sat quietly over supper, enjoying each other's company. They were young and in love and only too happy to be alone together.

The little house next to the towering red and white lighthouse was small but beautiful. The tall cliffs where both sat touched the sea and were in a perfect position to feel both the soft sea breezes and the full fury of the fiercest storms. No matter how hard the wind blew or the sea raged against the cliff, Harry and Martha always felt safe and snug in their cottage. Even when Harry had to climb to the top of the lighthouse to service the light, he was never anxious for his safety. After all, the lighthouse had stood on that very spot for nearly two hundred years, and no storm, no matter how strong, had been able to dislodge it from its place atop the cliff.

Over the years Harry had a front row seat to much of nature's majesty. He could see for miles and often watched a gathering storm approach until it broke to fling the waves against the cliffs sending spray all the way up to the top of the lighthouse before it blew itself out.

Harry was acutely aware of the importance of keeping the light burning to guide the many ships that passed through the narrow passage. He knew how treacherous that passage could be and was aware that before the lighthouse had been built, many ships had met their doom in that narrow and shallow passage. Because of that sad history, Harry was very conscientious about keeping the light shining brightly to warn the ships of their dangerous passage through the narrow channel.

Over the years, Harry and Martha had settled into a comfortable routine, content in their solitude and in the company of each other. Shortly after sunrise and a quick cup of tea, each took care of chores: Harry to the care and maintenance of the lighthouse, Martha to the care and maintenance of the household. They met mid-morning for a hearty breakfast and a time for prayer. Being so close to nature made them acutely aware of a powerful God, and over the years they drew closer to Him as they did to each other. They had come to rely on starting each day in prayer, asking for God's protection and His direction for their day.

Having only each other and a very occasional visitor for company, they came to rely on their times of quiet conversation with each other and with their God. It was a time of growing: growing together, growing in their faith, and growing in their service to those unseen sailors who worked the many ships that passed by their lighthouse. They often stood on the shore, watching the ships pass and imagining who was on board, where they were headed, and what their personal stories might be. They had no way of knowing the importance of their vigil and the part their lighthouse would play in the life of one of those sailors.

One day Harry was seated in his small cottage in a small town not too far from his beloved lighthouse. Having become too old to manage the chores necessary to keep the lighthouse working, Harry had turned its care over to another. Even though the light was now automated and no longer needed someone living on site, the work still required someone to oversee it twenty-four hours a day, seven days a week, and at Harry's advancing age, it was no longer possible for him to maintain that schedule.

Oh, Harry was not yet ready to give up on life, no sir, and although still very strong, his bones now felt the storms in a way they had not just a few years ago. And although the life had hardened him, giving him an uncommon strength of body and character, he was feeling the nibbling of old age at the edges of his body. *Mentally*, he was still that young man who had accepted the job of lighthouse keeper so many years ago and who brought his young bride to that solitary life atop the cliff, to live in communion with the sea and nature, but *physically* that was no longer true for him.

Harry had again settled into a routine, as was his nature, but it seemed to have little purpose and certainly none as important as his days as keeper of the lighthouse. He felt a need to "do something"—but what?

Christmas was coming in a few days. Harry had not felt much like celebrating in the two years since Martha had left him. Christmas seemed to be a futile affair, and as they had had no children, there was no family to come bursting in the door with grandchildren and all the happy chaos that accompanied the gathering of a family together during the holidays. So, he had done little other than attend church services on Christmas Eve and sift through the memories of Christmases past.

But not this Christmas, Harry declared to himself. This year he would rouse himself from his dreary state and get on with living. He was becoming too much like the Scrooge of the Dickens *Christmas Carol*, a man who thought Christmas was too much trouble to bother about. He might be alone, but there was a world out there full of people, and Harry determined to re-enter it with gusto.

His first thought was, What to do? Well, for a start, he could decorate the house, make it festive again. Somewhere, he still had the Christmas tree ornaments he and Martha had used every Christmas for most of their married life.

And he could put a wreath on the front door—make it look like someone lived there; make it welcoming. Not many people stopped to visit Harry these days, but who knew? Maybe if he made an effort, that would change. And perhaps there were other lonely souls out there, sitting alone on Christmas.

Thoughts spilled out of Harry's head as he became energized with his project. He put on his coat and hat, threw a scarf around his neck, and grabbed his gloves. He would walk the few blocks to town and see if he could find a tree and someone to deliver it. And a wreath—don't forget the wreath. That would be a start. There was a spring in his step as he closed the front door and hurried up the walk. He would ask the man at the Christmas tree lot if there were others in town who had nowhere to go on Christmas. Harry was not much of a cook, but there were lots of packaged products in the stores these days, and he was sure he could manage something. It would be better than a solitary meal eaten alone in an empty house—anything would be better than that. And besides, Christmas was a time of sharing, wasn't it? Harry would get back in the spirit of the season and begin sharing in the life of the town again.

Chapter 2

Harry found the town was more than ready for Christmas. There were decorations in all of the store windows. Houses had lights and decorations on doors, in windows, and in the yards. He saw candles in many windows and strings of lights on bushes and outlining the house roofs and windows.

Seeing the candles gave Harry an idea. *I was the keeper of the light for so many years, and lately I have been living in darkness, lonely and alone, while outside a world was going on without me. Martha would never approve of what I have been doing with my life, and I suspect neither would God. I am still here, there is still a world of people out there, and I think God must still have a job for me to do or He would have taken me home to be with my beloved Martha.*

So what should an old lighthouse keeper do now? pondered Harry. *Maybe a Christmas candle in my window would be a start. Let people know someone lives there and would welcome them in.* Harry remembered hearing the story of the purpose for the candles in a window when he was a child. Years ago, when houses were few and far between, people kept a lighted candle in their window at night to guide weary travelers to a place of refuge for the night. For years, Harry's light had guided people safely through a dangerous and narrow channel. Perhaps a light in the window of his house would serve to guide a lonely traveler to a place of refuge on land as his lighthouse light had done for those at sea.

Yes, thought Harry. *It's a good idea and a good start.*

Harry saw a parking lot filled with Christmas trees and a small trailer at the corner of the lot. There were lights inside, and Harry quickly walked into the lot to find the perfect Christmas tree. As he strolled the rows of trees, he wondered why choosing a tree was such a big deal. They were all beautiful once you had the lights and ornaments on them, but ever since he could remember, choosing just the right one had become a ritual of nearly every family, including his own. He remembered as a child running up and down the rows of trees, looking at each one until finally, his parents told him to just pick one so they could get out of the cold and back to their warm house. It was not a chore to be done in haste, and Harry smiled as he remembered being that small boy with the determination not to go home with anything but the most perfect tree available. Chuckling to himself, Harry critically examined each tree on the lot. Finally, sure of his choice, he knocked on the door of the trailer.

Harry told the man his choice and asked if someone could drop it off at his house. The man agreed to drop it on his way home as he said he had to pass right by. It would be no trouble at all, and it would fit nicely in the back of his truck.

Harry paid the man for the tree and asked where he could buy a wreath for his door.

"Try the flower shop at the end of the street," the man answered with a smile. "They have the prettiest wreaths, none of that artificial plastic stuff you see in some of the stores now-a-days...the real thing, with the smell of pine: real pine cones, holly berries and a bright red ribbon. That's what you want in a real Christmas wreath."

Harry heartily agreed and shaking the man's hand, thanked him and wished him a Merry Christmas.

"Oh, before I forget," Harry said, "are there any people who will be alone at Christmas? I have decided to open my house this year to anyone who is alone or has no place to go. Christmas is not a time to be alone and forsaken."

The man thought a minute and then looked up. "There is one man I can think of. Hasn't lived here too long, but I believe he's alone. Never seen him with anyone. He comes in for breakfast a couple of days a week. Don't know his name, but maybe Phil at the cafe might know. I think he lives at the old Harris farm just outside of town."

"Thanks for the tip," said Harry, and he headed toward the flower shop, then on to the cafe. A cup of hot chocolate sounded good before he headed home to start decorating his house.

Chapter 3

The flower shop was a Christmas wonderland. It was filled with wreaths, table decorations, poinsettia plants, Christmas cactus, tree ornaments, bows and ribbons of all sizes and kinds, and a number of candles.

Harry choose a wreath—a real one—with pine cones, red and green holly sprigs, and a big red bow.

That ought to brighten up the front door, he thought. And I'll get a big candle for the front window, one that will last until after Christmas.

Taking his choices to the front counter, Harry decided to ask the shop lady if there was anyone she knew who would be spending Christmas alone.

"I know of a young widow whose husband was killed in an accident just a few months ago. She has two small children, and I imagine it has been difficult for her. This will be their first Christmas without their Daddy, so I suspect it could be a sad one for them if they are alone. I don't think she has any family close by. Her name is Emily Johnson and the kids are Blake and Ann. They live in the yellow house across the street next to the grocery store."

Harry thanked the lady, paid for his purchases, and

headed for the cafe and that cup of hot chocolate.

"Merry Christmas, and thank you," said Harry as he closed the door to the flower shop behind him. He was on a roll now, and the Christmas spirit was back full strength. He had forgotten how exciting Christmas could be and how much fun doing something for someone else with no strings attached could be.

The cafe was warm, and he could smell cinnamon and apples. He found a booth, put his packages on one side, and slid into the other seat. Taking off his hat and gloves, he smiled at the waitress as she approached his table.

"What can I get you?" she asked with a smile.

"I'd like a cup of hot chocolate, please," said Harry, "and what smells so good?"

"That's Phil's special apple pie. We just took two of them out of the oven. Would you like a piece to go with your hot chocolate?"

"I sure would," said Harry. "It smells too good to pass up."

In just a minute or two, the waitress was back with a steaming cup of hot chocolate and a large slice of warm apple pie. Harry wasted no time in digging in.

He missed Martha's good cooking: her pies, cakes, breads, and cookies. And he missed Martha, but he was determined not to sit alone any longer feeling sorry for himself. There were people to meet, things to do, and Harry was going to get busy doing them!

When he finished his food, Harry caught the waitress' eye and motioned her over.

"I'm looking for a fellow who comes in here a couple of times a week for breakfast. Lives outside of town, alone I think. You see, I'm alone, and I've decided this Christmas to open my home to others who are alone and have no place to go for Christmas. I'd like to find this fellow and invite him for Christmas dinner at my house. Do you know him?"

"Yeah, I know him. His name is Able Patterson. He lives in an old brown farmhouse about a mile outside of town. He doesn't talk much about himself. Retired now, and as far as I know, living alone. At least I've never seen him with anyone else."

Harry thanked her for the pie, hot chocolate, and the tip about Able Patterson. His list was growing quickly. Harry had been so busy being alone, he had no idea there were so many others in the same boat. He chuckled at the comparison to being in a boat, and started home with his packages. If he was going to do a proper party for these people, he'd better make some plans. In the morning he would go visiting, but tonight he would get out the Christmas decorations he had saved from his years with Martha and see what else he might need to buy. And then he would see about Christmas dinner. He wondered how fast he could learn to cook when he remembered the wonderful pie he had eaten at the cafe.

I wonder if Phil might be talked into cooking a Christmas dinner for me. I'll go back tomorrow and talk to him about it. Maybe, if I tell him what I'm planning, he'll agree to help me out.

Smiling and full of plans and Christmas spirit, Harry opened his front door and began his active return to the life of the town—starting with Christmas.

Chapter 4

$\mathcal{D}$ecorating the tree was an emotional experience for Harry. He had never done it without Martha, and unwrapping each ornament brought back a flood of memories. But with an effort of will, he managed to keep himself in a positive mood. The final touch was the silver star that rested on top of the tree. Harry always put the star in place as a last touch just before they lit the lights. The tree was beautiful this year, just as it had always been.

I'll make this a happy Christmas for myself and as many others as I can, and I'll do it for Martha. She would like that, he mused, smiling at the thought of Martha, hands on her hips, a smudge of flour on her cheek, shaking her head each time Harry snuck into the kitchen to snatch another Christmas cookie from the growing stack on the kitchen table.

"Well, somebody has to taste test them," he always said as an excuse. Martha would laugh and tell him he was just a big kid at heart. Well, this Christmas he was going to live up to that description. Actually, he wasn't off to a bad start, but there was still a lot to do.

By the time Harry had finished with the tree, it was

dark outside, so he put the candle on the front window sill. As he lit the candle he thought how like a human life it was—full of bright promise at the start and then sputtering and flickering at the end, so quickly gone just like his life. Where had all the years gone? It seemed like only yesterday that he was a young man with the world at his feet and a lifetime to conquer it. Now, in what some called his "declining years," he was more filled with memories than purpose.

As he gazed out the window, he thought about the long life that God had given him and the many blessings He had sprinkled through it, but did that mean he was to sit in his chair and wait for the end to come? He didn't think so. He still had his wits about him, although it was getting more difficult to remember things—except for the past. That was still fresh in his memory. He could remember sounds: the crash of the waves on the rocks below; the howl of the wind; Martha as she sang a favorite hymn while kneading bread.

And the smells. He remembered those so well. Freshly baked bread just out of the oven, the salty tang of the sea air with a slight hint of seaweed and fish, freshly laundered sheets on the bed after being hung out to dry in the fresh air, and Martha's hair after she had washed it—a mix of soap and flowers.

Oh. Martha, my love! We had a good life, but it isn't the same without you. I know you are with our Lord, happy and at peace, but I miss our quiet times together. Forgive me if I get melancholy. You never liked to dwell on sad things but always found something to be happy about. You were the joy of my life, but until we can be together again, I shall endeavor to

*find what joy the world has to offer and to be of whatever use
God can find for an aging lighthouse keeper.*

With one more look at the candle burning brightly in
the window, giving off a faint scent of cinnamon, Harry
turned to the business of decorating the rest of the house.

I'm getting melancholy again, he acknowledged. *Plenty
of time for that when I don't have other things to do.* And he
opened the front door to hang the wreath.

*Tomorrow I'll visit the the Johnsons and Able Patterson.
That will be a start. If they agree to share my Christmas, I'll
see if Phil at the cafe can help me out with the food.*

Harry felt better than he had in several years. The
Christmas spirit had invaded his heart and awakened a
spirit of giving that was new and encouraging to him. It
reminded him of the kind of excitement he had felt as a kid
at Christmas time.

One more thing and I will be finished decorating, thought
Harry as he went back to the storage closet in the spare
bedroom. On the shelf he found a box labeled "nativity
set." Taking it down, he set it on the bed and gently opened
the lid. Inside, the pieces were each wrapped in tissue paper
and bubble wrap. This was his and Martha's favorite deco-
ration. It was an all-white nativity set with shepherds, ani-
mals, and wise men complete with camels. There was even
an angel that hung over the scene. Martha always put it
in a prominent place so it could be the focal point of the
decorations.

Harry wanted to display it just as she had done, so he
went outside and cut some pine branches to put on the
mantle over the fireplace. He wound a string of little white
lights through the pine so they would look like stars. Then

he gently placed each piece of the manger scene in place, just as Martha had always done. When everything was in place, he laid the baby Jesus in the manger between Mary and Joseph. The shepherds stood at a respectful distance at one side of the mantle with the donkey and the cow in between. On the other side, farther away, were the three kings and their camels, traveling toward the Christ Child to pay homage to Him with their gifts.

Stepping back, Harry took a moment to admire the scene and bask in the wonder of God's greatest gift to man—His Son. How special the memory of that gift made this celebration of Christmas.

Now for a cup of hot chocolate before I got to bed as a reward for a job well done, thought Harry as he headed for the kitchen to warm the milk. *I'd better get some sleep as tomorrow will be a busy day. It's only three days until Christmas and counting.*

Chapter 5

Harry was awake early the next morning. He hopped out of bed and took a quick shower. After shaving and combing his hair, he dressed quickly and headed for the kitchen to fix a hearty breakfast.

His usual breakfast was a bowl of cereal and a cup of coffee or tea, but today he wanted something more substantial to carry him through the busy day ahead. Besides, he was really hungry. That was unusual, but this was promising to be an unusual Christmas, so why not go all the way and have pancakes with syrup and bacon. He'd try that new mix that you just measured out and added water. It sounded simple. He'd see how good pancakes could taste where you just added water. But no matter, anything would taste good today!

He got out a frying pan and a bowl and put the water on to heat for coffee. He'd need the extra energy it always gave him. Now for the pancakes. He measured out the powder and added the water. So far so good. He melted a bit of butter in the frying pan and poured three bits of the batter into the pan. Harry watched for the bubbles to appear on the top of the batter just as Martha did when she made him pancakes for breakfast. Before long, there they were—little bubbles forming on the top of each pancake. Harry carefully inserted a spatula under the first one and flipped it over. Almost perfect. One side dropped on top of the pancake next to it, but Harry moved it over, and the second and third flipped without a miss. He poured himself a steaming mug of coffee while he waited for the pancakes to finish. The aroma of the bacon coming from the microwave told him it was ready. He piled it on his plate; added the pancakes; and carried the syrup, the pancakes, and his coffee to the table.

Before eating, Harry bowed his head for his morning talk with his God. It had been his and Martha's habit all the years of their marriage to begin each day in prayer. It seemed to set the tone for the day, and things seemed to go more smoothly when they started their day talking to God. Today was a day Harry hoped would go smoothly. He would need guidance and wisdom in reaching out to strangers. He didn't know these people or how they would react to a stranger inviting them to his house for Christmas. He would seek God's guidance for the day.

Heavenly Father, Harry prayed, *thank you for the marvelous gift of Your Son and for this season of remembrance. Help me to do You honor in what I am attempting to do this Christmas. You have sent many blessings my way through the years: a godly woman to be my wife and helper, a job I loved, and time and a place to grow in knowledge of You. I have been thoughtless these last two years. In my grief, I have forgotten Your order that we love our neighbors. I have stayed shut in my house with my memories, unaware of my neighbors or their needs. Forgive me for taking so long to remember that*

I need to be about Your work. Help me today as I approach these strangers. Help me to extend a hand in friendship to them and open their hearts to Your love for them expressed through me. Guide my words, Father, and help me to extend a genuine offer of love and comradeship to each of them. In Jesus precious name I pray. Amen.

After his prayer—offered with the knowledge that God answers prayer—Harry set about making his pancakes disappear as quickly as possible.

Pretty tasty. Not bad at all! he thought as he chewed happily. When his coffee mug was empty, he cleaned up quickly and headed for the door.

First stop Able Patterson's house. He's the farthest out of town. The Johnsons are closer to town, and if everything goes well, I can stop at the cafe and have a talk with Phil about helping me with the food for Christmas dinner.

With his plan in place, Harry bundled up and headed for his car. As he left the house, he noticed the first flakes of snow were starting to fall.

It looks like we may have a white Christmas, thought Harry. *Perfect*!

Chapter 6

Harry had no trouble finding Able Patterson's house. About a mile outside of town, he saw a brown farm house with a mailbox that had the faded name *Harris* on it. Painted in white paint above the faded letters was the name *Able Patterson* in shaky letters. Harry turned the car into the driveway and pulled up in front of the house. It looked quiet, but he saw a light on at the back of the house.

Probably in the kitchen, he thought as he got out of the car. *Well, Lord, wish me luck, and I wouldn't mind some leading in how to approach him and what to say. But, Your will be done.* With that, Harry knocked on the door.

A few minutes later he heard shuffling footsteps. The door opened, and a thin man with a grey beard and very blue eyes opened the door.

Harry smiled and prayed one more quick prayer: *Help me now, Lord, to say the right things to this man who is also Your child.*

"Hello! My name is Harry Long, and I live in a cottage in town. I know this might sound strange, but I have been alone these past two years, and I decided this year I didn't want to spend Christmas alone again. I am looking for some people who would like to share Christmas with me at my house. I wonder if I might extend such an invitation to you, if you have no other plans of course."

Able Patterson stared at Harry for what seemed like an hour, although it was probably only a minute or so. His blue eyes searched Harry's, probing deeply into Harry's soul. Harry kept his eyes fixed on Able's and smiled. His heart was beating wildly as he waited for a response. Finally, Able smiled and opened the door wide.

"Come in and have a cup of coffee, and we'll talk about it," he said.

"Sounds good to me," said Harry with a sigh of relief. *At least I'm in*, he thought. *The rest is up to You, Lord.*

They headed for the kitchen. It was sparsely furnished, but functional. The usual appliances and a small table and two chairs stood against one wall. It was warm, and Harry felt comfortable. Anxious to get to know this man, Harry thanked him for the steaming cup of coffee and sat down in the extra chair.

Able refilled his cup and sat across from Harry. He seemed friendly, but puzzled, so Harry set about explaining himself and his plan for sharing Christmas with his neighbors.

"My wife died two years ago," Harry began, "and I've been getting used to being alone, *if* that's possible. I've spent the last two years mostly alone, feeling sorry for myself, I suppose, while the world has gone on without me. My Martha would never have stood for that, so I decided this year to get out of the house and do something. I remembered the happy Christmases of the past and saw no reason for this one to be a sad and lonely one. I don't think that is what God intended in this special season for remembering the gift of His Son to the world. I decided to see if I could find some people in town who might be alone like me and invite them to share Christmas with me. I realize we don't know each other, but I understand you might be alone too, and I wondered if you might consider my invitation."

Harry took a deep breath and looked at Able. Able sipped his coffee, still with that quizzical look on his face.

"Why would you want to spend Christmas with a bunch of strangers?" he asked. "Seems kind of odd to me."

"Well," began Harry, "I didn't want to be alone again this year. I know others in town have families and will be busy with them. I don't want to intrude on a family get-together, and I thought perhaps there were some others in town who would be spending the holiday alone, like I have been doing these last two years. I don't know about you, but I don't think that is how Christmas was intended to be spent—alone. It's not much of a celebration when it's just you and the empty house. Will you at least think about it?"

Able stared at his coffee cup for a while, thinking. At last he looked Harry in the eye and spoke.

"I don't know you, and you don't know me, but your offer is a kind one. I've gotten used to being alone, and I don't mind it. I like to read, and I have my garden in the nice weather. Never had time for a garden until I moved here as I spent most of my life at sea. But I thank you for your invitation. I don't see what harm it would do to share your Christmas. What do you have in mind?"

Harry's mind had gotten stuck on Able's comment about spending most of his life at sea.

"I'm sorry," said Harry with a tinge of excitement in his voice. "You said you spent most of your life at sea. May I ask what you did?"

"Sure," said Able. "I worked the freighters carrying coal to the Far East. I traveled these waters most of my life, and decided to settle here when I retired. I always liked this part of the country when I was able to visit."

"Now that's quite a coincidence," said Harry. "You see, I was the keeper of the lighthouse on the point for thirty-five years. My Martha and I, we lived on the point and kept that light shining so the ships would have safe passage through the channel. It was a good life, and we were happy there. Many times we stood on the cliff watching those ships pass, imagining who was aboard, where they were headed, and what their stories might be. And now you tell me you were on one of those ships. That's amazing!"

Able chuckled, warming to the conversation. "It's a small world, so they say, and in this instance it appears to be so. So you're responsible for keeping that light lit. Many's the time we passed through that channel in rough weather, grateful for that beacon of light shining in the storm. We knew we could count on that light, and it never failed to show us the way. I'm pleased to be able to thank you for keeping that light bright. I know it saved us many times from going aground in a storm. That channel can be treacherous."

"That it can," agreed Harry, also warming to this old seaman. He felt a bond growing between them. *Thank you, Lord, for bringing me to this man.*

Able was quiet for a while, and then smiled at Harry. "I'd be pleased to accept your offer for Christmas. What do you have in mind and how can I help?"

"Well," answered Harry. "I'm still thinking things through. The idea was a bit of a last minute plan, but dinner for sure. Perhaps an evening together, some Christmas music, some food, and some time sharing memories of happy Christmases. I'd just like us to be able to share each other's company and to make a day that is supposed to be a celebration just that. Being alone at Christmas when others are with family and friends is not my idea of a celebration. What do you say? I'm open to any suggestions."

"My mother made the best eggnog at Christmas. I think I remember how to make it. How about if I bring a jug of that to the party. And I have some old Christmas records: Bing Crosby and *White Christmas* and all. I could bring them if you have a way to play them. I'm not much for singing, but I am a good listener, and it could help set the mood," suggested Able, warming to the project.

"Sounds great!" Harry agreed. "I have my old phonograph in the attic. Never knew why I kept it, but never got around to getting rid of it. Now I know why. I'll get it out, dust it off, and make sure it's in working order. How does five o'clock sound?"

"Sounds good," said Able, smiling. "Where's this party to be?"

"My house is the white cottage with red shutters just past the post office on Main Street. I wanted to stay close to the sea, and on clear days, I can just see it in the distance. It reminds me of happy days spent on the cliffs above the sea in my lighthouse. I guess the sea gets into your blood, and once there, you can't bear to be too far from it."

"I'll agree to that," said Able. "That's one of the reasons

I settled here. I don't feel the roll of a ship under my feet, but I can still go down to the beach and sit on the rocks and listen to the surf and the screams of the gulls as they dive for fish. The rhythm of the waves and the smell of the sea quiets me and gives me a peace I don't find anywhere else."

"I agree," said Harry. "The sea is a marvel, so peaceful one minute and a raging fury a short time later. I have always loved the changing personality of the sea. It's like a living, breathing thing, and over the years I came to love it. Now I can't bear to be far from it either.

"Well, I've imposed on your hospitality long enough, I must get on with my to-do list. Thank you for the coffee and the conversation. I'm so glad you have accepted my invitation, and I look forward to seeing you Christmas night."

"I'll be there with my eggnog and my records," said Able with a twinkle in his eye. "Thanks. I guess I wasn't thinking about Christmas until you came. Now that I have something to look forward to, I'm finding that old Christmas spirit is starting to wake up. I look forward to your party. See your then."

Able walked Harry to the door, and the two men shook hands. Harry felt the stirring of a kinship with this man. Their common love of the sea had created the beginnings of a bond between them.

"Goodbye, Able, and thank you for humoring a crazy old man's idea. I'm looking forward to seeing you again and to tasting that eggnog. See you Christmas night."

Harry walked to his car whistling a Christmas tune and started the engine. The snow had continued to fall and now there was a light dusting covering the ground. One down, and one more to go. He backed the car out of the driveway and headed for the Johnson house back in town.

Harry's success with Able Patterson had given his heart a boost, but he knew it did not ensure things would go as well at his next stop.

Nothing ventured, nothing gained, he told himself, and he turned his car toward town.

Chapter 7

The yellow house next to the grocery store was small, but neat. Harry parked his car in front of the house and got out. There were toys scattered on the porch, and a red ball in the bushes next to the steps. Taking a deep breath, he offered up a quick prayer for guidance and headed up the path to the house.

He climbed the steps and crossed the porch. Pausing for a moment to gather his thoughts, he knocked on the door. He could hear the voices of children inside. A woman's voice quieted them and the door opened.

She was small with dark hair and a pretty face. She looked tired and wary of this strange man at her door.

"Can I help you?" she asked.

"I hope so," said Harry. "My name is Harry Long, and I live on the other side of town. This might sound a bit strange, but I would like to invite you to my house to spend Christmas with me and some of my friends. You see my wife died two years ago, and I have been alone for the last two Christmases. Martha wouldn't like to see me moping around the house by myself. She was always busy and happy. She couldn't abide anyone feeling sorry for themselves. Always said activity was the best medicine, and she was right as far as my life is concerned. Would you let me come inside for just a minute and explain my idea to you. I'm perfectly harmless, and although I know it sounds strange for someone you don't know to invite you for Christmas, I just couldn't stand the thought of another lonely Christmas, just me and my memories. I thought there must be some others who needed to be with friends at Christmas."

He waited while she considered whether to let him in or not. *Please, Lord, let her know I mean her no harm.*

"All right," she said. "You look pretty harmless. My name is Emily Johnson and these are my children, Blake and Ann. Say hello to Mr. Long, children."

"Hello, Mr. Long," they chimed in unison before running off to continue whatever game they had been playing.

"Please sit down, Mr. Long, and tell me more about this idea of yours. I must say, it did strike me as unusual, to say the least, asking a complete stranger to share Christmas with you."

"Well, as I said, my wife died several years ago. We had no children, so I have no family. I was the lighthouse keeper for thirty-five years at the lighthouse on the cliffs at the edge of town. My wife and I were happy there for those years and didn't miss not having a family because we had each other. Now that she is gone, I realize that having children would mean I still had family, but that was not in God's plan, and I accept that. It does not mean, however, that I have to be alone. I realize by staying in my house I chose solitude for these past two years, but that is not the way I want to continue. Martha would never stand for it, and so to honor her memory, I decided to see if I could find some people in town who might also be lacking in family and would like to have the option of spending Christmas with others. It is supposed to be a festive time, and I felt it would be easier to feel festive if there were others to share it with me.

"I understand you are a recent widow. Although you have your children, I thought this Christmas might be a difficult one for you and that perhaps together, we could put our loneliness aside and make a celebration out of it. What do you say?"

Harry waited while Emily thought over his offer. He could see the conflict in her eyes. She didn't know him, but his story sounded plausible. Should she take a chance? Christmas would be quiet without her husband. The children had been told Daddy was gone and was not coming home again, but she was never quite sure they understood. They were so little—five and six. Death was difficult for a child to comprehend. It was difficult for her to comprehend, when she thought about it! She didn't think she'd every really get used to not hearing her husband's voice as he returned from work at night.

"Emily, I'm home. Where are the kids?" He'd always say the same thing as soon as he came through the door. As soon as they heard his voice, the children ran to greet him, leaping into his arms. He'd grab them and lift each one high into the air to their squeals of delight. Emily smiled as she remembered the happy sight, and then suddenly she was back in the present, and he was gone forever. She fought the tears that wanted to fill her eyes again. She thought she had cried herself dry, but each day there seemed to be a new supply, an endless supply. Would this sorrow never end?

Harry saw the emotions cross Emily's face as she fought the tears. He could identify with her sorrow. Although hers was a more recent loss, his own was no less sharp. Even after two years, the pain of his loss was still a shock to him. Sometimes it hit him so hard it nearly took his breath away.

Help me to reach out in love to this dear lady, Lord. Tell me what to say to ease her hurt, Harry prayed.

"I understand your hesitation," Harry said. "You have only just met me and don't know me, but would you think about it? It would be a joy to hear the laughter of children in my house and to know that others are sharing this special time of year with me. I thought we could share dinner and some fellowship Christmas evening. I have invited Able Patterson, a retired seaman who lives alone on the other side of town, and he agreed to come after some hesitation like I sense you are feeling. He thought I was a bit daft at first, as I suspect you are thinking as well, but I assure you my offer is genuine and heartfelt."

Emily laughed. "You're right. I did think you were a bit crazy when you first told me about your idea. I'm sorry, but you must admit coming out of the blue like that, that it could seem a bit strange."

"I'll agree to that," admitted Harry. "I thought it was a bit crazy myself when I thought of it at first. But the more I considered it, the more right it seemed. I believe God meant this to be a celebration of His gift to the world to be remembered happily each year. It certainly was a celebration that first year: angel choirs, kings with gifts, shepherds visiting, a new baby. Sounds like a celebration to me."

Emily laughed again. "Mr. Long, you do have a way with words. I'll think about it and let you know tomorrow, How can I get in touch with you?"

Harry prayed silently: *Thank you, Lord, for giving me the right words.*

He wrote his phone number for Emily on a piece of paper. "I'm going to go ahead with my preparations in the hope that you and your children will accept my invitation. Thank you for your hospitality, Mrs. Johnson. I'll be waiting for your answer."

That went rather well, Harry thought as he walked back to his car. He saw two faces in the window as he opened his car door, and he waved. The children waved back and then disappeared. *It's up to you now, Lord,* Harry prayed as he started his car and headed for Phil's cafe.

Chapter 8

The first stop after the Johnson's house was the café to talk with Phil. After that, Harry would go to the grocery store and get some party provisions.

The café was reasonably quiet, probably because it was too late for the lunch crowd and too early for dinner. It might just be a good time to have a few minutes of Phil's time.

The same waitress greeted Harry again and asked if he had come back for another slice of apple pie.

"No," laughed Harry. "But it was worth coming back for. I wondered if I could talk to Phil for a few minutes—that is if he's not too busy right now."

"Let me check," and with that, she disappeared into the kitchen.

A minute later, Phil came out, wiping his hands on a towel. "Hello, Harry. What can I do for you?"

"Hi, Phil. Thanks for giving me a few minutes. I have something I want to ask you. You know I've been a bit of a loner since Martha died—well, worse than that. I've been a veritable hermit! Anyway, that's over now. I don't want to spend another Christmas alone—too depressing. And I thought there might be others in town with no family to speak of who would also have to spend Christmas alone because they have no one to share it with. I thought I'd open my house to anyone with nowhere else to go, and we'd see if we could make a celebration out of it—more the way God meant it to be, don't you think?"

"Not a bad idea, Harry, but where do I fit in?" asked Phil, smiling.

"Well," said Harry cautiously, "you can probably guess that it was Martha who was the cook in our family, not me. Oh, I could probably rustle up a meal, but it would hardly qualify as *festive*. I wondered if you would consider cooking the meal for us. I'd furnish the food, of course, and pay you for your time—whatever price you set is okay with me."

Harry waited while Phil thought it over. "What time do you plan to have this dinner?" he asked.

"I thought about five o'clock. Would that work for you?"

"I think it would," Phil answered with a smile. "I could start the meat in the morning if it's turkey you have in mind, and then come in later in the afternoon to finish the rest. I can bake the pies the day before, and you can just warm them in the oven while you eat, if you like. How would that work?"

"If it wouldn't interrupt your Christmas celebration with your family, that would be fine."

"No interruption I wouldn't be glad of," said Phil with a smile. "By late afternoon I'm ready for a break from the noise and confusion in the house with five grandkids and their parents. It would be soothing to come into the café where everything would be quiet and finish up your dinner. It's a deal, and don't worry about paying me for my time. Call it my Christmas present to all of you. I'm only too glad to help out. It's a nice thing you're doing."

"This is just great, Phil. As soon as I get a head count, I'll get the rest of the fixings. Right now, I'm off to the grocery store to get a turkey before all the big ones are gone. I want one big enough to give everyone some leftovers to take home. Leftovers are some of the best part of a turkey." With a wave of his hand, Harry hurried out of the café and headed toward the grocery store across the street.

Harry headed straight for the back of the store to the meat counter. As he passed through the produce department, an older lady bumped the corner of a table of oranges with her cart. An avalanche of oranges rolled to the floor and proceeded to roll in all directions. Her face got red, and she looked as if she might cry.

Harry hurried over to help. "Looks like those oranges have a mind of their own," he said with a smile as he stooped and began picking them up.

"I can't thank you enough," she said, still looking distressed. "I'm so embarrassed. Just look at the mess I've made."

"Well it serves them right for making those kind of towers with round fruit. It's just an accident waiting to happen," replied Harry, putting the last orange back onto the table. "You look familiar to me. Do I know you?"

"Maybe," she answered. "My name is Mary White, and I've been the fourth grade teacher in town for years—that is until I retired last year. Since then I haven't done much other than miss the children."

"What about your family?" Harry asked. "Surely they

visit you."

"Oh, the children were my family. I never married, and I have only one sister who lives all the way across the country. Besides, she has a family of her own and is busy with them."

Harry's eyes began to sparkle. "So you're alone then?"

"Yes, I'm alone. I don't mind it most of the time, but in the winter it's hard for me to get out and about, and it gets lonely."

"Well, Miss White, I have a proposition for you."

Mary White's eyes widened, and she looked at Harry strangely. "Whatever do you mean?" she asked.

"Let me introduce myself first. My name is Harry Long, and I was the lighthouse keeper for thirty-five years. My wife and I lived on the cliffs and tended that light for most of our married lives. After I retired, Martha—that's my wife—lived only a few months. She died two years ago. Since then I've stayed home alone, nursing my grief. I went out only when I had to, and I have to tell you, although I still miss Martha sorely, two years of sulking alone is enough. I decided this Christmas to get back to living again. Martha would never have approved of my sitting alone in the house this long. She was a doer, my Martha— and a happy one at that.

"Anyway, I thought it might be an idea to see if anyone else in town was going to have to spend Christmas alone and to invite them to share it with me at my house. I'm not much of a cook, but Phil at the café has agreed to cook the dinner, so it will be worthy of a celebration. I'd be honored it you'd consider joining me and a few others on Christmas night for dinner and a little celebration afterward. What do you say, Miss White?"

"Oh, Mr. Long, you're an answer to prayer. I'd be honored to join you for dinner. What may I bring?"

"Just bring yourself, Miss White. Say, you don't play the piano by any chance, do you?"

"I do, Mr Long. It's a requirement for grade school teachers to be able to play piano. It helps with the singing we do in class. Would you like me to play some Christmas carols?"

"I would indeed, Miss White. That would be splendid and will add immeasurably to the festivities. It will help drown out my singing voice that is somewhat lacking in all ways except volume."

"Oh, Mr. Long, I'd be delighted to play. Are there any children coming? I could make them some presents to open since it's Christmas. I have a knack at crafts, and a house full of supplies left over from twenty-plus years as a teacher. I'd be more than happy to make something appropriate."

"There are two, a boy and a girl—about five and six, I believe. Their father was killed several months ago, and this will be a difficult Christmas for them. I have not heard yet if their mother has agreed to come, but I am praying that she will say yes."

"I will pray as well that she will say yes, Mr. Long. You have a generous heart."

"Thank you, Miss White, and since you are going to be a house guest of mine, please call me Harry."

"Thank you, Harry, but only if you agree to call me Mary."

"It's a deal, Mary," said Harry with a big grin. "It's sounding more like a party every minute. Dinner will be at five o'clock and my house is the white cottage with red shutters just past the Post Office on Main Street. Do you need a ride?"

"No, Mr. Long...or...I mean...Harry...I don't. I live just behind you on Maple Drive. It won't be any walk at all, in fact, we're practically back-door neighbors."

"Well, what do you know about that!" exclaimed Harry. "Here I have a whole town full of potential friends and didn't even know it. That goes to show you what a recluse misses out on, stuck in the house all alone and moping all day long. I'm glad to be over that, and I'll bet Martha is glad to see me gettin' on with living. I'm on my way to talk with the butcher to buy the biggest turkey he's got. See you at five o'clock Christmas night, Mary."

They waved at each other, smiling. "See you then, Harry, and thank you again."

Well, Lord, you're making this quite a party, aren't you? Thank you for that. Help each of us find Your special message in the Christmas celebration this year. And now, to get that turkey.

Harry waited his turn at the butcher counter. When the butcher asked him what he could get him, Harry answered, "The biggest turkey you've got. I'm having a special Christmas party, and I need a big one!"

"I've got a twenty-four pounder, if that's big enough," said the butcher. "What's this big party anyway?"

"Twenty-four pounds sounds about right. I've been moping around the house for two years since my Martha died, and you might say this is my "coming out party." I've invited some folks from town who would be alone this year, and we're getting together to make our own party.

Christmas is supposed to be a happy celebration, not a time for sadness and loneliness. Don't you agree?"

"I do indeed," said the butcher. "That's real nice of you, Mr. Long. We need more people with the kind of Christmas spirit you're showing. Might make this world a happier place for all of us. When do you want to pick up your turkey?"

"How about December 24th? Phil is going to cook it for me, and I can take it to him that morning so he has time to do whatever one does to get a turkey ready—that is, if it's not frozen."

"No, sir. None of my Christmas turkeys are frozen— fresh only, that's my motto. Tastes better, and saves hours thawin' 'em out. December 24th is fine. See you then, Mr. Long."

Harry left the grocery store with a bag of cookies, some apples, several loaves of bread for stuffing, celery, onions, and a big smile. He started to whistle, something he hadn't done in years. As he passed people on the street, they smiled, and some even said hello.

Whistling has become a lost art. More people ought to get back into whistlin', thought Harry. *It sounds friendly and happy and makes people smile which makes them happy too. Spreads happiness around, and that's a good thing.*

I'm hungry. It's been a good day's work. I need to get home in case Emily Johnson calls to let me know if she and her kids are going to join us. I'm sure Mary White would like to see some kids at the party. And I'm in need of some food. Those pancakes are long gone, and my stomach's growling.

Harry continued whistling all the way to his house, up the walk, and through the front door.

# Chapter 9

*E*arly that evening, the phone rang. Harry put his newspaper down and went to answer it.

Let it be Emily, Lord, and let her say yes!

"Hello."

"Hello, Mr. Long? This is Emily Johnson."

"Hello, Emily. It's nice to hear from you."

"Well, Mr. Long, I've thought about your offer, and I've decided to accept. It won't be much of a Christmas for the children without their Daddy, and your party might take their minds off him. Thank you for your offer."

"It's my pleasure, Emily. Christmas wouldn't have been much for me if I hadn't made a change, and your coming with the children will be really special. There is something missing at Christmas if there are no children, and your two will add to the festivities, I'm sure. Do you need a ride?"

"No, thank you, Mr. Long. I have a car. Is there something I can bring? I'd like to contribute to the party in some way."

"Well, let me think. I have dinner covered, the tree is up and decorated, Mary White is going to play piano for us so we can sing some Christmas carols, and Able Patterson is bringing eggnog and some Christmas records to play during dinner. I'm open to suggestions."

"How about if I bake some Christmas cookies? The kids and I make it a Christmas ritual to do that, and I can make some extra. I could make enough so everyone could take some home."

"I think that's just the ticket, Emily," said Harry. "I don't think we have forgotten anything, unless you can think of something else."

"Not at the moment," said Emily. "I'm on my way to the store to buy cookie ingredients. I'll just pick up a few extra items and start baking. I bake, and the kids decorate. It can get messy, but they enjoy it so much, and a mess can be cleaned up. It's something I hope they remember as a happy time at Christmas, and maybe it will help all of us not to be too sad this year."

"I know the loss of a spouse takes time to get over, if you ever can say you really get over something like that, but I have learned the hard way that life must go on for the living. You have your children to care for, so you have had to force yourself to go on even when you might not want to do so. I admire you, Emily. I know it must be difficult at times, but with time it will get a little easier. I will pray for you. Remember, God is there for you whenever you need Him."

"You know, Mr. Long, since my husband died, I have been angry at God. How could He do that? Take a husband and a father away from a young family? I haven't reached out to Him, but have accused Him of not caring. I suppose that's wrong, but I have been so alone and confused. I guess my faith is not as strong as it should be for someone who has gone to church all her life. I must not have learned much in all those years."

"Emily, it is always difficult when we are sorely tested, as you have been, but the choice is always to choose God or not. It takes us time to make that choice sometimes, but it is there nevertheless. I remember hearing someone say once, 'When you've been knocked down you have two choices: to stay down or to get up.' Gettin' up took me two years, but I'm up now, and I can tell you, it's a lot better up here than it was down there. Grief takes each of us a different way, and we each have to find our own way back. But when you're ready, God will be there waiting for you, and whether or not you know it, He's right beside you now, holding you up when you can't stand on your own, guiding and directing you. Look, He led me to you, and you are going to help me make Christmas what God meant it to be—a celebration."

"Thanks, Mr. Long. I needed a pep talk like that. I'll try to remember what you've said when I get depressed."

"In the meantime, Emily, remember there are those of us in town who are here to be God's hands and feet. We will be there for you and will try to help out when you need it. Can I ask a favor of you?"

"What would that be, Mr. Long?"

"Two things," said Harry. "First, please call me Harry. And second, let me know if and when you need help, no matter what it is. I'd be happy to do whatever I can to ease things for you. I know what you're going through, and maybe together we can help each other get on with living. Will you do that? I mean, let me know when you need help—no matter what it is, even if it's just a shoulder to cry on, someone to talk to, or a leaky faucet that needs fixing? Is it a deal, Emily?"

"It's a deal, Harry. Thanks."

Harry hung up the phone and smiled. *Spunky lady, that one! Now, let's see what I've got. Able, Mary, Emily and the two kids, and me. That's six people so far. I've got the turkey, stuffing fixings, Phil's cooking dinner with pies, Able's bringing eggnog and records, Mary's playing the piano and making gifts for the Johnson kids, and Emily's bringing cookies for everyone. All I need to do is buy potatoes, vegetables, cranberry sauce, and rolls; and we're all set. I've got enough dishes for six, but I could get a bright red table cloth and some Christmas napkins at the party store. Candles on the table would be a nice touch. I can use Martha's mother's candle sticks. Martha would like that.*

Tomorrow I'll pick up the turkey and the rest of the things, drop them off at the café, and go home to do some last minute cleaning. I'd better make sure everything is cleaned and polished before the big day. Don't want to be doing that at the last minute.

Thanks, Lord, for waking me up and showing me neighbors who needed someone. This just might be one of my most memorable Christmases, thanks to your whispering the idea of a party into my ear. I'll bet You had that guest list all ready and waiting. Well, I'm glad You did, and glad You found a use for an old has-been lighthouse keeper. Just because I don't keep the lighthouse light any more, I still have to let my own light shine, just like You said to do. I've been keeping it under a bushel basket, and You said not to do that. Well, I've thrown off that basket, and I'm ready to shine again, just like that Christmas candle in my window. Help me to help each of these dear friends who is going to share Christmas with me to light their own candles and let them shine as well. In all things, let Your will be done in my life. In the name of Him whose birth we celebrate, Amen.

With that, Harry headed up to bed. It had been a busy, but productive, day. He would sleep well tonight, and then tomorrow the final preparations for the Christmas party would be finished. Harry was more excited than he had been in years.

I'm starting to feel like a little kid the night before Christmas, he chuckled, *and that's not bad at all*!

Chapter 10

$\mathcal{H}$arry was up early the next morning. Determined to get everything done in good time, he ate a quick breakfast while making himself a shopping list. He was also determined not to forget something, necessitating a return trip to the store. Satisfied he had not forgotten anything, he bowed his head in prayer: *Heavenly Father, You are so gracious in Your love for Your children. As Your child, I have felt Your protection and Your direction so many times in my life. I ask for that direction now as I complete preparations for the celebration of the birth of Your Son with these dear people to whom You have led me. Help this celebration be one of love and praise to You, and let it be meaningful to each one here. Let it minister to the secret needs of each heart that we each may return home strengthened by our shared experience. Thank you for Your watchful eye on my life, and for Your gracious continued use of whatever time and talents You have given me. As in all things, may Your will be done. I ask these things in Jesus name, Amen.*

Harry always felt a kind of peace after his time of prayer, no matter how brief.

It's so easy to get too busy to spend just a few quiet minutes talking to God, he reflected thoughtfully. *It's funny how the world can so easily push what is often the most important part of my day aside. When I let that happen, I find I am caught in what almost seems like a whirlpool, swirling faster and faster as I rush to keep up, when just a few minutes at the start of my day can put everything into perspective. Amazing how smoothly it all goes then. I can thank Martha for getting me in the habit of daily morning prayer. It was her idea, and a habit I am pleased to say has stuck.*

His coat, hat, and scarf on, Harry pulled on his gloves and closed the door behind him. Shopping list in his pocket, he headed for the grocery store to pick up the rest of the supplies for dinner and to deliver the turkey to Phil.

The store was more crowded than usual with lots of last-minute shoppers, but the mood was festive rather than stressed. Harry filled his shopping cart with potatoes, vegetables, rolls, cranberry sauce, and the huge turkey—and headed for the checkout.

In less than half an hour, he was on his way across the street to Phil's cafe. Phil was in the kitchen as Harry put the box of supplies on one of the tables.

"Here you are, Phil. I hope this is everything. I also have bread, celery, and onions for the stuffing. I can't tell you how much I appreciate your doing this for me. I am afraid my efforts would not have made dinner much of a celebration. Oh, yes. I never made arrangements to come and get the food. What time should I be here?"

"No need for you to leave a party to pick up dinner. I have to drive back home anyway when I'm finished. I'll just drop it off on my way home. That way *you* can stay home and play host."

"Wow, Phil! That would be great. I'll owe you a big favor for all this." said Harry, his eyes twinkling with anticipation.

"I'll keep that in mind" answered Phil. "Dinner's at five o'clock, right?"

"Right," said Harry, "and thanks, Phil. You're a real Christmas angel. See you on Christmas."

"The turkey, fixin's, and I will be there at five o'clock sharp," answered Phil. "Now I've got to get busy with today's lunch special. See you later, Harry."

With that taken care of, Harry headed for the party store to find a table cloth, napkins, and some candles for Martha's mother's candlesticks.

The store was packed with people, and things looked pretty well picked over, but Harry found a bright red table cloth that someone had put in with the wrapping paper. Napkins were still plentiful, and he found some with holly leaves in the corner.

Candles were at the front of the store. As he headed toward the cashier, Harry noticed a shelf of tiny lighthouse Christmas ornaments. He stopped to look and decided that putting one at each person's place at the table would be a nice touch and would be a gift they could take home as a little remembrance of the day. He picked out six and headed for the line at the cashier.

By the time Harry got home, it was lunch time. He made a peanut butter and jelly sandwich and poured a glass of milk. Time was of the essence now. He browsed through the newspaper while he ate and then got busy putting the house in order.

Some dusting and vacuuming done, Harry set the table

for the next day's dinner. The table cloth was a good fit, and the candles gave it a nice touch. He put the lighthouses around at each place and stood back to admire his work.

Not bad, if I do say so, he admitted, smiling. Now for the kitchen and bathroom and I'm done. A quick dinner and I should be finished in time for Christmas Eve service at church. That always puts me in the Christmas mood.

Chapter 11

The church looked lovely. The altar was lined with poinsettia plants in memory of family members, and there were candles and pine branches everywhere. A huge tree at the front corner was ablaze with tiny white lights, and the organ played Christmas hymns softly as people filed in and found seats.

Harry bowed his head for a moment after he found a seat and just soaked in the peaceful scene. Then the organ raised the volume and everyone stood as the opening notes of "Joy to the World" filled the church.

The message was brief, but appropriate, and gave Harry the idea that he should read the Christmas story from the Gospel of Luke after dinner. It would set the mood nicely, and they could sing some carols afterward. It might be a good ice breaker, letting people get comfortable with each other. He would have to make sure Mary played some songs Blake and Ann would know, so they could join in too.

Maybe he should take the baby Jesus out of the manger and let one of the kids put him in place as they hear the Christmas story. Yes, that would be a nice touch and make the kids feel they were participating. One could put the baby in the manger, and the other could put the angel on the hook when he read the part about the shepherds and the angels.

As he walked home, snowflakes began to fall again and gave the whole scene a hushed feel—almost as if it were in anticipation of some great event. As Harry turned into his yard, he saw the flickering light of the candle in his window.

Yes, my Christmas candle is doing the job, all right. It looks homey and welcoming, just as I had hoped. Frontier homes had the right idea, to keep a light in the window to welcome weary travelers. Too bad we live behind locked doors glued to TV sets. Fellowship is becoming a lost art.

Harry watched the evening news and had a glass of milk and a cookie before heading up to bed. It was nearly midnight when he climbed into bed, and as he closed his eyes, he heard the chimes in the church tower striking midnight.

Merry Christmas, Martha. I hope tomorrow will be a day to remember, and one to make you proud. I miss you. And Harry was asleep less than a minute after closing his eyes.

Chapter 12

Emily Johnson finished her shopping and headed home with the kids for their Christmas ritual of baking cookies. They usually saved it until closer to the actual day for several reasons. First, it kept the holiday mood going and seemed to help build the sense of excitement for the kids, but most important it ensured there would actually be cookies left for Christmas. With two little kids and one very overgrown one, cookies had a way of disappearing rather quickly in the Johnson house.

Emily pulled into the garage, she and the kids piled out of the car, packages in hand, and headed for the kitchen.

"Get your coats and hats off, and I'll meet you in the kitchen for the bake-off," she said with a smile.

The kids deposited their grocery bags on the table and raced to the front hall—to hang up their coats? Probably not, she smiled. They'll be on the floor or on the steps just like always. No matter how often she told them, "Hang up your coats," they still seldom wound up in the closet. *Oh, well, they are just kids*, she signed and began unpacking the groceries.

By the time the children found their way back to the

kitchen, Emily had everything ready and recipes in hand.

"Are you ready to start?" she asked.

"Yep," said Blake while Ann dragged her step stool over, a sure sign that she also was ready to start.

"Which ones first, Mommy?" Ann asked as she started reaching for a nearby bowl and spoon. "Can I work the sifter? It's my turn this time. You promised!"

"Yes, you may, and I did promise. Blake can help me measure. Lets get started. We'll do the roll-out ones first, and the dough can cool in the refrigerator while we bake the others. Then after lunch, we'll roll it out, and you two can decorate them."

Baking cookies with two small children was boisterous, messy, and loads of fun. They always laughed and sang and had a wonderful time. Emily was thankful that they were able to enjoy simple things together. She hoped she was building happy memories for the children, and maybe they would do the same thing with their own children some day.

The afternoon passed quickly with lots of laughter, but Emily found her eyes wandering to the kitchen door, looking for her husband's face peeking in to check on what they were doing. He always put up the outside lights while they baked but popped in as often as he felt he could get away with it to snatch a warm cookie. "To keep up my strength," he would say with a grin, disappearing back outside. The kids always thought that was hilarious and usually dissolved into fits of laughter with each sneak visit from Dad.

Emily sighed and forced her thoughts back to the present. There would be time for quiet remembering when she was alone. Right now it was important to make Christmas a happy time for Blake and Ann. Interestingly, she found herself getting excited about Harry Long's impromptu Christmas party. She was really looking forward to it. She would wear her red dress, the one her husband liked so much, and dress up the kids as well. It would be fun to be with other people for a Christmas celebration rather than at home alone with her memories, fighting tears.

Chapter 13

*M*ary White had been busy ever since she met Harry Long in the grocery store. She thought about a gift to make for the children on her way home, and by the time she had her groceries put away, she had decided.

She had made a Noah's ark with cloth figures for the kindergarten class at school, and it had become a favorite plaything. There was not time to make an ark, and anyway, the ark was not part of the Christmas story. But she could make figures for the manger scene, and a manger would be easier to fabricate than the ark. She could use popsicle sticks and cover them with dry moss that she used in her flower pots. She was sure she had some straw somewhere in her craft supplies, and it could be glued to the inside. Yes, that would work nicely.

She found her box of fabrics, and choosing some for the figures of Mary and Joseph, she got started right away.

I think I'm going to have as much fun making these as I hope the children will have playing with them.

By late afternoon she had finished the figures of the holy family and had started on some shepherds and sheep. She would sew some leftover white and black yarn in loops to make the sheep look fuzzy, and a pipe cleaner bent into the shape of a shepherd's staff would be safer and more durable than a stick. In the morning she would make a stable for the figures—and an angel. She mustn't forget the angel!

Mary had been practicing Christmas carols in between sewing as it gave her fingers a rest from the cramped position sewing imposed. She enjoyed playing the piano. She had not done it as often since she retired but made a promise to herself to start again. It gave her pleasure and made the house seem less lonely. Maybe she should consider giving piano lessons to the neighborhood children. It would give her something to look forward to, and she could work with children again. Yes, that was an idea to consider after the holidays. The income would supplement her pension as well.

When Mary looked at the clock, she realized it was later than she had thought.

I'd better put this away for tonight. I can finish in the morning, but I'd better decide what to wear tomorrow. I can't just put on any old thing if I'm going to a party.

Mary climbed into bed, weary but happy. After saying her prayers with a special blessing for Harry Long and a prayer for each of the others she had been told would be coming to Harry's Christmas party, she closed her eyes and was quickly asleep.

Chapter 14

Able Patterson woke on Christmas morning surprised to find he was filled with anticipation.

"I'm really lookin' forward to this evening," he mused. "Imagine that! An old codger like me gettin' excited about Christmas. Well, I'll be jiggered!"

He chuckled as he got dressed and then headed downstairs to put the coffee pot on the stove. A quick breakfast and he would be ready to get started on the eggnog. He had to get it just right.

After several taste tests, Able was satisfied. He poured it into a nice jar and put it in the refrigerator until it was time to leave for Harry Long's party.

Five o'clock dinner, he'd said. I'll get there just a bit earlier, so Harry has time to try out my Christmas records, Able decided as he sat on the couch, pulling the carton of record albums closer. He spent several hours going through them, picking out the Christmas ones and remembering the many favorite songs on some of the others.

I just might have to see if I can get me a used record player. It'd be nice to hear some of these old songs again. There must be lots of people like Harry who have one stuck away someplace that they never use any more.

His chores done, Able pushed back in his recliner to take a short nap before getting ready for the party.

I wonder if I need to wear a suit, he thought as he began to doze off. *It's a party, after all. Guess a body should dress up a bit for the occasion.*

Chapter 15

Christmas morning arrived bright and sunny with a sparkling blanket of snow on bushes and the ground.

Harry busied himself with a few last-minute details and then spent a while in prayer for the evening and for each of those who would share it with him. So far everything had gone splendidly, and he wanted to ensure it would continue. He was already feeling a comradeship with these people, and he hoped it would spread among the others.

It's Your party, Lord, and You're the real host. I place these dear people in Your hands, Harry closed. And confident as always of answered prayer, he turned his thoughts to other things.

The afternoon passed quickly, and soon it was time to get dressed for the party. Harry put on his dark blue suit with a white shirt and a red tie.

Pretty festive looking, Harry, old boy! he mused, assessing himself in the bathroom mirror then heading for the stairs.

It was getting dark outside, so he lit the lights in the living room and dining room and then lit the Christmas tree lights.

I always loved the sight of our Christmas tree all lit up and decorated, and the way the pine smell fills the room. One last touch, and I'm ready for my guests, thought Harry as he went to the window and lit the Christmas candle. He stood for a minute looking at the darkening sky and the soft cover of snow on the yard. Everything was so quiet and peaceful. *Soothing to the soul,* he thought as he turned to check the dining room table once more before his guests arrived.

In a short time, his doorbell rang. Able Patterson was the first to arrive as promised with a large jug of his special eggnog and a stack of records under his arm.

"Able, it's wonderful to see you. Come in, come in. Let me help you with those things. I'm anxious to try this special recipe of yours."

Harry carried the eggnog into the kitchen and led Able to the record player set up in the dining room.

"Let's try one of your records and see if this old thing still works."

"I came just a mite early for just that reason," said Able. "I thought you might want to look over what I brought."

"Good idea," said Harry. "Able, these look wonderful. Let's try Bing Crosby; he's always been a Christmas favorite of mine."

They stood listening to the strains of "White Christmas," each lost in his own memories.

"Music sure brings back memories of Christmases past, don't it?" asked Able with a far away look in his eyes.

"It sure does, Able," said Harry. "Good memories."

The door bell rang again and broke their reverie. Harry headed for the door and found Mary with a large box wrapped in bright Christmas paper and tied with a large bow.

"For the Johnson children," she said.

"Oh, Mary, that looks wonderful! Come in. I don't suppose you'd tell me what's in it?" Harry asked with a smile.

"No, Harry, I won't tell you what's in it. That would spoil the surprise now, wouldn't it?"

"Yes, I guess it would, Mary, but there was no harm in trying, was there? Come and meet Able Patterson. Able, this is Mary White. She was the fourth grade teacher here for over twenty years."

"Hello, Mary, it's nice to meet you," said Able as he reached to shake Mary's hand.

"My pleasure, Able. Have you lived in town long?"

"No, ma'am, only about four years. I used to work the freighters and always liked the look of this town when we passed by, so I decided to settle here, and it lets me stay close to the sea. The sea gets in your blood, and once it does, you can't be happy far from it."

"I agree with that, Able. I love the sea and can't imagine living far away from it either."

Just then the door bell rang again. Harry directed Able and Mary to the living room while he went to answer the door.

"That's probably the Johnsons. Put the present under the tree, Mary, and we'll let it be a surprise for the kids."

Harry opened the door and welcomed Emily and her children. The children entered quickly and in short order took in the dining room table, the tree, and the rather large box under it. Their eyes were wide, and they were visibly excited.

Emily had several bags which Harry helped her carry into the kitchen.

"I don't know when you would like me to pass these cookies out, but you can let me know when to do it," said Emily. "Thank you, Harry, for this evening. The children have been on pins and needles all day waiting for five o'clock."

"I'm glad you decided to come," said Harry. "And by the way, you look lovely in that red dress—very festive."

Emily blushed, but the smile on her face was a happy one. *Lord, give this dear lady Your peace this Christmas, and make this holiday one of healing for her*, prayed Harry silently. "Let's join the others, Emily, and I'll introduce you"

Mary and the children were already acquainted and talking animatedly while Able watched with an amused look on his face.

Introductions made again, Harry told everyone about Able's special eggnog recipe and offered everyone a cup. They each complimented him on the tasty treat and visited comfortably for a short time. The door bell rang again.

"That's probably Phil with our dinner," said Harry. "I must admit I cheated some and asked Phil from the café to do the cooking. I'm afraid my talents don't lie in the cooking direction. He graciously offered not only to cook the dinner but also to deliver it as well."

Harry opened the door, and Phil handed him a large platter covered in foil.

"Here's the bird," he said. "Careful, it's pretty heavy. I'll go back to the truck and get the rest."

"I'll give you a hand," said Able while the ladies took the foil off the turkey and put it on the table. Emily lit the candles and called the children.

With the food all delivered, hot and steaming, Harry put the pies in the oven to warm and got everyone seated. They poured drinks and complimented Harry on his table.

"It looks so lovely," said Mary.

"Thank you, Mary. I am so pleased you all agreed to accept my invitation. This is a very special Christmas for me. I'd like to say a thank you to God. Would you all join hands?"

The little group joined hands and bowed their heads while Harry prayed: "Thank you, Lord, for this special season celebrating of the gift of Your Son. And thank you for these dear people who are sharing this Christmas celebration together. I pray that You will make this a special time for each of us, in Your own special way. Thank you for your provision and for this meal which we are about to share together. Amen."

"Amen," responded the others.

"Able, how about putting on one of your Christmas records to give this party a little atmosphere?"

"Can do, Harry," said Able as he got up and chose a record.

"Can we cut the turkey now, Mr. Long? I'm hungry!" said Blake, scooting forward in his chair.

"Blake!" said Emily. "That's not polite."

"We certainly *can* carve the turkey," said Harry. "I'm hungry, too, and I hope the rest of you are as well. We want to eat while everything is still hot."

The turkey was carved, the dishes passed, and the meal was spent in pleasant conversation as the strangers slowly became friends. Mary was good at including the two children in the conversation, and after the pies had been devoured and everyone confirmed they could not eat another bite, Harry blew out the candles, and they returned to the living room.

Harry asked Mary to play a few Christmas carols and the little group gathered around the piano. What resulted was hardly the sounds heard from church choirs, but the singing was boisterous, and the laughter genuine. After most of the old favorites had been sung, they ended with a rousing rendition of "Jingle Bells."

"I'd like to continue the evening by reading the Christmas story from the Gospel of Luke," said Harry as everyone found seats and got comfortable. "There is a nativity set that Martha and I used every Christmas. I have taken out the baby Jesus and the angel and thought perhaps Ann and Blake would like to put them in place when I read about them in the story."

"Can I do the angel part?" Blake asked. "I think angels are cool. They can fly, you know."

"Yes, you can," Harry replied, "and Ann can put baby Jesus in the manger." He handed each of the children their figures, opened his Bible to Luke, Chapter 2, and began to read:

> In those days Caesar Augustus issued a decree that a census should be taken of the Roman world. This was the first census that took place while Quirinius was governor of Syria. And everyone went to his own town to register.

Joseph also went up from the town of Nazareth in Galilee to Judea, because he belonged to the house and line of David. He went there to register with Mary, who was pledged to be married to him and was expecting a child. While they were there, the time came for the baby to be born, and she gave birth to her firstborn, a son. She wrapped him in cloths and placed him in a manger, because there was no room for them in the inn.

And there were shepherds living out in the fields nearby, keeping watch over their flocks at night. An angel of the Lord appeared to them, and the glory of the Lord shown around them, and they were terrified. But the angel said to them, "Do not be afraid. I bring you good news of great joy that will be for all the people. Today in the town of David a Savior has been born to you; He is Christ the Lord. This will be a sign to you. You will find the baby wrapped in cloths and lying in a manger.'

Suddenly a great company of the heavenly host appeared with the angel, praising God and saying, 'Glory to God in the highest, and on earth peace and good will to men.'

When the angels had left them and gone into heaven, the shepherds said to one another, "Let's go to Bethlehem and see this thing that has happened, which the Lord has told us about."

So they hurried off and found Mary and Joseph and the baby, who was lying in the manger. When they had seen him, they spread the word concerning what had been told them about this child, and all who heard were amazed at what the shepherds said to them. But Mary treasured up all these things and pondered them in her heart. The shepherds returned, glorifying and praising God for all the things they had heard and seen, which were just as they had been told. (Luke 2:1-20)

Blake and Ann had placed their figures in place right on cue, and everyone was quiet when Harry finished the familiar story, each with his or her own thoughts about the meaning of God's greatest gift to mankind.

But the story only held the attention of the children for a moment before the lure of the large, brightly wrapped box drew their gaze. It was obvious they were most curious about it, but neither dared ask about it. Mary watched with amusement and finally said, "I wonder what's in that big box under the tree."

The children's attention was instantly riveted on Mary.

"Is there a card?" asked Harry. "Perhaps that will give us a clue."

Mary bent down to look as both children squirmed in anticipation. "Well, what do you know." she said. "It says *Blake and Ann Johnson.*"

The children whooped and dove for the box. Paper and ribbon was soon scattered on the floor and the box lid was off. As the children pulled out the manger and the figures of the nativity scene, their eyes shone.

"Is this for us?" asked Ann.

"Yes, it is," said Harry. "Mary made it especially for you, so you would have your very own Christmas family."

"Thank you, Mary" said Blake. Ann was already putting the baby in place in the manger.

"Mary, what a wonderful present, and it was so thoughtful to think of a present for the children. Thank you." Emily's eyes were moist with tears as she watched her children acting out the story they had just heard.

While the children played quietly in a corner of the room near the tree, the others settled down to visit.

"Do you all know the story of the Christmas candle?" asked Harry. "If not, I'd like to tell it to you."

Many years ago when this country was young and homes were few and far between, someone started the custom of putting a lighted candle in the window at night to welcome weary travelers. That light could be seen for miles across the prairie and promised a refuge for the night to anyone who needed it.

One Christmas, it was particularly cold, and a young family had become lost while trying to reach Grandma's house for Christmas. The town they sought was nowhere in sight, and they knew they had become completely lost in the cold dark. The wife was expecting a baby and had become exhausted by the trip. Their little girl was running a fever, and the father was at a loss as to how to find a warm place for his family for the night when he saw a light in the distance. He led them toward that light, and eventually he came to a cabin near a small wood of pine trees. Their wagon had broken down, and the horse could not carry them all.

When they got closer to the cabin, a barking dog alerted the family inside who took them in, giving the weary parents their own bed for the night. They nursed the sick little girl and even went to town to get a doctor for her.

While she was recovering, the rescuers learned the lost family's grandmother and her husband had hosted needy people for a Christmas party for years. Now that the grandfather was gone and the grandmother was alone, her son's family was coming to spend Christmas with her so she would not be lonely.

So, a surprise party was planned as a Christmas surprise for Grandma. As soon as the little girl felt better, the new friends took the family to Grandma's house in the nearby town. They spent the day together and they had a lovely Christmas.

Shortly before dinner, they got another surprise when the new baby arrived a bit early. But as in all things, God's timing was perfect as He brought them the extra Christmas surprise of a new baby boy.

In honor of their Christmas rescue, both families always kept a candle in a window at Christmas time—just in case any weary travelers needed to know a safe refuge was waiting nearby.

"I decided to put a candle in my window this year," explained Harry. "I was the keeper of the light on the cliff for years, letting that light shine over the sea, and I thought I could do the same on land to let people know there is a warm welcome in this house any time they need it."

"That's a lovely story, Harry, and a wonderful idea about the candle. I will put one in my window when I get home tonight," said Mary.

"We'll do the same," said Emily.

After a while, Able said, "Harry, since you and I talked the other day about your being the lighthouse keeper all those years, I've been remembering something that happened while I was on one of those freighters.

"We were about an hour out from the channel trying to beat an approaching storm when all hell broke loose. By the time we neared the channel, that ship was tossing and bucking in waves as big as any I'd ever seen. The wind was howling so fierce that even with safety ropes, we didn't dare go on deck. The captain had us batten down the ship, and we settled down to ride it out as best we could. I got to tell you, I was mighty scared. I knew we were nearing that channel, and in *that* storm, there were no guarantees that we would make it through.

"That lighthouse light was both a welcome sight *and* scary, because it meant we were ready to enter the channel. I was prayin' my heart out and so were most of the crew. I watched out one of the port holes as that light went by, and somehow we made it through the channel. I've had a fondness for that lighthouse ever since. It was like a beacon tellin' us that everything would be okay—and it was."

"I remember that storm, Able," said Harry. "It started just before dark and blew all night. I stayed up top to make sure that light didn't go out, because I knew it would be disaster for any ships in the area if it did. Martha kept me plied with hot coffee and soup to be sure I stayed awake. I saw a ship pass through sometime during the night, and I said a prayer for their safe passage to their destination, but I never dreamed I'd meet someone who was on it. Imagine that!"

"Well, I have to admit that storm changed my life," admitted Able. "I was never much of a prayin' man before that storm, but like some folks do when they're in a real tight spot, I made a bargain with God. I said if He'd get me through that channel and safe in to port, I'd make an effort to get to know Him better. He kept His part of the bargain, so I've done my best to keep mine. There's nothing like a tough trial to bring you to the foot of the cross, asking for help. I'm just glad God was there to hear me."

"God is always there to hear us when we ask earnestly," said Harry. "I had the chance to see God's power lots of times during my years at that lighthouse and to know His provision all through my life. I must admit after Martha died, I drifted a bit and doubted some, too. But before long, I realized that death is a part of His plan, just as living is, and I came to terms with it.

"This Christmas was a turning point for me," continued Harry, "because I decided since I was still here, God must have a purpose for me, and I needed to get up and get out and discover what it was that He had for me to do. This celebration is a kind of 'coming out party' for me, you might say."

"I guess it's my coming out party too," said Emily. "It's been hard for me and for the children, losing a husband and a father, but after Harry's invitation, I realized I had reached a turning point, just like he said. At first, I thought to refuse his invitation. I didn't know him or any of the people he said he had invited. I felt awkward about coming to a party when I was still so sad. I still cry easily and don't know when or if I will ever really get over Tom's death, but I understand now that I must make the effort. I've decided as soon as both children are in school, I'm going to go back to school and finish my teaching degree. I need to get a job, and I need something to do that will bring in some money and yet will allow me to be home when the children are. Teaching will do that, I think. And I think Tom's life insurance will last until then if I'm careful."

"Emily, I think that's a wonderful idea," said Mary. "I loved my years as a teacher. But if you are waiting so the children will be in school to start, I'd be more than happy to help out babysitting. Your children are delightful, and I must admit I've been missing the children since I retired. They were all like my family, and it's been more lonely than I thought it would be since I stopped teaching."

"That's very generous of you, Mary. I can't pay you much, but it would enable me to start sooner. I realize that I have to get my life back on track, and the sooner the better for both me and the children. I would love it if you could help out. Thank you. I have come to realize I can't do it all by myself, and I will just hurt the children and me by trying. Perhaps God sent you dear people to me, and I am thankful to Him for that and to Harry for being the first answer to my prayers. Thank you all, and thank you for this lovely evening. The children and I have something in the way of a little thank you gift for each of you. Children, would you get the bags in the kitchen?"

Blake and Ann returned, each with a bag, and at Emily's direction, passed out tins of cookies for each of the guests.

"We made these," said Ann.

"And I decorated the best ones," offered Blake proudly.

"How about another glass of eggnog, and we'll all sample this cookie treasure," Harry suggested. Everyone agreed, and he and Able went to the kitchen to get the drinks.

The children and Emily were complimented on their cookies, and Emily told them to say their good nights and thank yous to everyone. They thanked Harry and Able, and each gave Mary a big hug which brought tears to her eyes.

"Good night, children," she said. "I hope you will let me come and visit you soon."

"Oh, yes," both children agreed. "Come and play tomorrow."

"Tomorrow is as far ahead as they think," laughed Emily. "Well, maybe not tomorrow, but soon, if that's all right with Mary."

"It sounds just fine," she answered.

"Now we need to head home and get you two into bed, or I'm going to have a couple of sleepy grumps on my hands tomorrow. Come along children. And thank you for a wonderful evening, Harry."

"Don't go without taking some of this leftover turkey," said Harry. "I got a big one so everyone could take some home, and I expect you to do just that, or I'm going to be eating turkey until Easter. Come on everybody, and load up."

They all trooped into the kitchen, and in a short time the turkey was divided.

"Save the bones for soup," said Emily. "That's often the best part."

"I'm not much of a cook," said Harry. "Why don't you take them?"

"I'll do that if you all agree to come to our house this weekend to help us eat it. What do you say?"

"Oh, do come," said Ann. "We can have another party."

They all agreed, and one by one they headed for the door.

"Don't forget to take your lighthouse ornaments from the table," said Harry. "Those are yours to keep as a remembrance of tonight, and I hope this might be just the first of many happy gatherings."

And it was.

Epilogue

It's been twelve years since Harry's impromptu Christmas party.

Blake Johnson just graduated from high school and is off to college in the Fall to become an architect. Ann has one more year of high school and then wants to become a nurse. Emily went back to school to get her teaching degree and has become one of the best-loved grade school teachers in town.

Mary White still lives in her house, tends her garden, and teaches piano to the town children. Blake and Ann call her "Grandma Mary," and she and Emily have become close friends.

Able Patterson passed away five years ago, followed by his best friend, Harry Long, two years later. They shared their love of the sea for many years and became active in getting a senior center built for the town's growing number of senior citizens.

Best of all, in memory of Harry's story about the Christmas candle that he told at his Christmas party that first year, every house in town puts a candle in a front window from the first of December through Christmas to wel-

come any strangers that may be passing through town at
Christmas.

Printed in the United States
127876LV00001B/1/P

9 781932 966626